**THAT'S LIFE
PictureStories**

BOOK 7
Tax Time

Tana Reiff

LAKE EDUCATION
Belmont, California

Cover Design: Ina McInnis
Text Designer: Diann Abbott

Library of Congress Catalog Number: 94-079115

ISBN 1-56103-782-6

Printed in the United States of America

1 9 8 7 6 5 4 3 2 1

The Marcianos

■ **Frank Marciano** *He owns a grocery store and has something to say on every subject.*

■ **Marge Marciano** *She listens to everyone's problems and knows how to help.*

■ **Ernesto Marciano** *Frank's father retires from life until he meets Rosa Esteban.*

■ **Gina Marciano** *The Marcianos' daughter is very much her own woman.*

■ **Doug Kelly** *He and Gina Marciano have a life plan that works for them.*

The Adamses

■ **Walter Adams** *Keeping up with a growing family has its problems.*

■ **Ruth Adams** *She manages to keep her cool through all of life's surprises.*

■ **Pat Adams** *A 13-year-old learns something new about life every day.*

■ **Tyrone Adams** *At 16, does "Mr. Basketball" really know it all?*

The Estebans

■ **Carlos Esteban** *Since his wife's death, he's both father and mother to his children.*

■ **Rosa Esteban** *Carlos's mother doesn't let age stand in the way of happiness.*

■ **Rick Esteban** *He finds that it's easy to get in trouble when you're 16.*

■ **Roberto Esteban** *This 14-year-old boy is making big plans for his future.*

■ **Bonita Esteban** *Growing up means having to learn about all sides of life.*

The Nguyens

■ **Nguyen Lan** *She can handle being a single parent in a new country.*

■ **Nguyen Tam** *At 4, he asks his mother why he has no father at home.*

Don Kaufman works on his income tax return

Don Kaufman, the mail carrier, is working on his income tax return. He remembers that Benjamin Franklin once said, "Nothing is certain but death and taxes." If Kaufman had to choose one or the other, he'd rather pay taxes.

"While working on my income tax return," Kaufman says, "I got to thinking how fast money goes. Walter Adams and I were talking about that the other day."

Why don't people like to work on their income tax returns?

Where does the money go?

Ruth Adams has just bought groceries. She is putting the food away. Her husband, Walter, discovers that there is only $4 left until payday. That isn't very much money.

"What am I going to do?" Walter asks.

Ruth jokes with Walter. She isn't surprised that there is so little money left. She knows how much food costs.

"We must make some changes around here!" Walter says.

What kinds of changes would Walter like to see?

Walter learns about food prices

Walter helps Ruth take the food out of the bags. He can't believe how high the prices are.

"Why do you pay so much?" Walter asks Ruth.

"Because that's what Frank and Marge charge," Ruth answers. She buys her food at Frank and Marge Marciano's corner store. Frank and Marge are their friends.

Ruth knows how high food prices are. Since there is little she can do about it, she isn't upset about the prices. But Walter is!

What do you think a person can do about high food prices?

Supermarkets charge less

Walter asks Ruth if she can buy food that costs less.

"At the supermarket, maybe," answers Ruth. She does her big grocery shopping there. Prices are often lower at the big supermarkets. Ruth shops at Frank and Marge's store when she needs just a few things.

"I *like* Frank and Marge," says Walter. "But their prices . . ."

Where do you buy your food? Why do you shop there?

Walter has a great idea

Walter says that he could save money if *he* were to do the grocery shopping. He would shop around for low prices. But when Ruth agrees to the idea, Walter isn't so sure of himself. He has never shopped for the groceries by himself. But it's too late for Walter to back out.

"It might help to have a fresh player in the game," Walter says.

**Do you think that Walter can do
the shopping any better than Ruth?**

Walter needs help

Frank and Marge Marciano are working in their store. Frank finds some boxes with the old price on them. The price has gone up, but the boxes haven't been marked up yet. Tyrone Adams didn't finish changing them all. Tyrone, Walter and Ruth's son, works in the store after school and on Saturday.

Suddenly, Frank sees Walter sneaking in the store.

"I need help," Walter whispers.

Why do you think that Walter is whispering?

Frank explains unit pricing

Walter points to some stickers on a shelf. He asks Frank what they mean.

Frank tells him that they are unit pricing stickers. They show how the prices work out for smaller amounts. Suppose a quart bottle of soap costs $1.28. The unit pricing sticker shows that the soap in the quart bottle costs 4¢ an ounce. The soap in the pint bottle costs 96¢, which is 6¢ an ounce.

How can unit pricing help you save grocery money?

Say that again?

Walter doesn't understand how unit prices work. He still doesn't see the use of unit pricing stickers.

"They help you to *compare* prices," Frank explains. "This sticker tells you that an ounce in a quart bottle costs 2¢ less than an ounce in a pint bottle."

Walter can save money in the long run if he buys the quart bottle.

Do you think that larger sizes are *always* better buys than smaller sizes?

Walter is just taking notes

Finally, Walter understands unit pricing. A quart bottle of soap only *seems* more expensive than a pint. The unit price shows that you really save money by buying the large bottle.

But Walter doesn't want to buy the large bottle. He is just taking notes now.

"You mean you're not *buying* anything?" cries Frank. Frank thinks that he should charge Walter for standing around in the store!

Do you most often buy large sizes or small sizes?

Home at last

By the time Walter gets home, it is very late. He has been out shopping for food.

"I went to five stores," Walter explains. "I was comparing unit prices!" He tells Ruth that, for most things, prices are lower at the Co-op store.

Ruth doesn't find this very exciting. But she can see that Walter enjoyed comparing prices.

**Is it a good idea to compare prices at
five stores to find the best buys?**

It must be beginner's luck

Walter tells Ruth more about his shopping trip. Frank and Marge's prices are higher than the big market prices.

But Frank and Marge's prices are worth it to Ruth. Their store is nearby, so it's easy to shop there. To Ruth, that is worth money, too. Now she wants to know how much Walter spent for food today.

"I spent $55.17 at Safeway," Walter tells her.

Why can a big store charge less for food than a little store does?

Walter has really done his "homework"

Ruth wants to bring the groceries inside, but Walter has more to say.

"The same groceries at Superthrift would cost $53.29," Walter goes on. "The cost at Giant would be only $52.94."

"Hey, that's great," says Ruth. "But, Walter, where are the groceries?"

Why does Ruth ask where the groceries are?

Smart shopping takes longer

Walter tells Ruth that the Co-op store came in first. The groceries there came to only $52.01!

"Walter, let's get the groceries," Ruth says again.

"I'll have to go out for those after dinner," Walter tells her. "I didn't have time to *buy* anything. But now I know where to shop."

"Walter!" laughs Ruth. "You're too much!"

How do you think Walter did on his first shopping trip?

Kaufman carries a heavy load

Kaufman's mailbag is heavy today. People are sending in their tax returns, and refunds are coming back. It is tax time. Kaufman is also carrying the market newspapers with all the food ads and coupons to cut out. Walter saves those food coupons like baseball cards. He takes them to the store to get lower prices on food.

Do you save coupons?

Now Ruth sneaks into the store

Ruth walks into Frank and Marge's store. Frank thinks that Ruth has come to see her son, Tyrone. But Ruth doesn't want Tyrone to know that she's there.

"Give me three chickens in plain brown paper!" Ruth whispers. She wants Walter to think that she got the chickens at another store. Chickens are on sale there for 69¢ a pound. Frank and Marge's chickens cost $1.39 a pound, but Ruth thinks they are much fresher.

**Do you think that fresher chickens
might be worth the extra money?**

Ruth stays under cover

Then Marge walks into the store and says hello to Ruth.

"Shhh," says Ruth. She doesn't want Tyrone to hear.

Frank explains that Ruth is supposed to be buying chickens somewhere else. Walter wanted her to save money by buying chickens on sale.

"Walter is trying so hard to save money," says Ruth. "But he is driving me nuts!"

How do you think that Walter is driving Ruth nuts?

Time is money

Walter was in here the other day. He dropped about 1,000 coupons all over the floor.

I turned the food shopping over to him. I don't think he knew how hard it is.

How is he doing?

He's too busy comparing prices to **buy** any food!

He checks prices Friday night. Then I go out Saturday and buy the food. We **are** saving money, but it takes so much time.

Frank saw Walter just the other day. That's when Walter dropped all his food coupons on the floor. Walter is learning that it takes work to shop for food.

Ruth explains that Walter checks prices on Friday night. Then she buys the food on Saturday.

"We *are* saving money," says Ruth, "but it takes so much time!"

How much time are you willing to spend comparing food prices?

Saving money isn't easy

"Sounds like the Adams family is really into saving money," Marge says.

"We are," says Ruth. "But sometimes I wonder if it's worth the trouble."

Ruth would like Frank to finish wrapping the chickens. She has to go home and work on their income tax return.

Frank jokes that Walter should do that. Maybe he could compare taxes and find a cheaper country!

What ways do you have to save money?

Walter's do-it-yourself shelves

Walter is building new shelves for the hall closet. But the shelves are too short. First, he drew his plan on graph paper. He figured four squares to an inch. Each inch on the graph paper equals one foot of the shelf. But Walter has made a mistake.

"This graph paper has *five* squares to an inch!" says his daughter Pat.

When Ruth comes in, Walter blames his mistake on the graph paper!

What is the real reason for Walter's mistake?

Refunds bring smiles

Ruth asks Pat to clear her things off the table. She needs room to work on their income tax return. Ruth learned about taxes in an evening class she took. She also learned about budgeting—how to spend and save money wisely.

Walter wants to get a lot of money back from taxes this year. The people he works with always talk about their big refunds. He doesn't want to be left out.

What would you do with a big tax refund?

Ruth knows her stuff

To do the tax return, Ruth needs to have proof of how much money they earned last year. Both Ruth and Walter save the pay stubs from their paychecks. These stubs show how much money they earned from working. Their bank statements show the amount of interest their money earned in the bank. The W-2 forms show how much they earned from working and how much they paid in taxes for the whole year.

Next, Ruth needs proof of what they spent. But the sales slips seem to be missing.

What is the first thing you should do before working on your taxes?

Accidents will happen

Ruth needs the sales slips that they keep in a shoe box. These show how much money they spent on medicine. They might get some of that money back in a tax refund. But where is the shoe box? It was on the closet shelf.

"I'd better go see if the garbage truck has come by yet," says Walter. It seems Walter got carried away when he was cleaning out the closet!

When was the last time you threw something away and wished you hadn't?

The Adamses have their problems

Walter really got into the comparison shopping thing. Not a bad idea, if you have the time. He and Ruth are doing their own taxes this year. But they had a problem. Walter had thrown away a shoe box full of sales slips! I wish I had seen Walter digging in the garbage can to find it!

Kaufman knows that Walter has been doing a lot of comparison shopping. It's a good idea, but it takes time.

Kaufman also knows that Ruth and Walter are doing their own income tax return this year. But they had a problem. Their shoe box full of sales slips had been accidentally thrown away. Walter had to dig in the garbage to find it.

**Besides comparison shopping, how else
are Ruth and Walter saving money?**

Finders keepers

Walter has found the shoe box of sales slips in the garbage. But everything is a mess. He finds Ruth's little black book. She wrote down the trips to the doctor's office in this book. They can subtract part of the cost of the trips from their taxes. So Ruth keeps track of every mile.

Do you think that keeping a trip book is a good idea?

There's a first time for everything

Walter isn't sure that they should try to do their tax return themselves. They have never "itemized" before—listed their deductions in detail on the long tax form. "Deductions" are dollar amounts that won't be taxed.

"We can handle it," says Ruth. She took an evening course to learn how to do the taxes. If they need help, they can call the IRS (Internal Revenue Service). The call won't cost them anything.

Who do you think did the Adamses' taxes last year?

So far, the taxes are easy

To do the taxes, Ruth and Walter must find out how much money they made. First, they add up their incomes from their jobs. Then they add the interest they made from their savings accounts. The interest from First National Bank and the Credit Union adds up to $48.

Why do you think banks pay interest on savings accounts?

Every little bit helps

Ruth and Walter have good reasons to itemize their deductions this year. With the birth of the baby, they paid a lot of medical bills. Some of this money can be subtracted from their gross income. They can also subtract the money they paid in interest on their house loan. They can deduct the taxes on their house, too.

By listing all these things on the long tax form, Ruth and Walter can save money on their taxes. All those who are buying a home should itemize their deductions.

When do you think it's worth the trouble to itemize deductions?

Ruth adds up the deductions

Ruth has already itemized all the things that they can deduct from their income. The money they paid for all their medical bills, the house taxes, and the house mortgage interest are their deductions. And Ruth can subtract *some* of the money that they paid for medical bills.

The Adamses know that the more deductions they have, the less taxes they will have to pay.

Why do people who pay interest on their mortgage pay less taxes?

Better late than never

April 15 is the last day to send in tax returns. Kaufman wonders why so many people wait until the last minute. All that mail at once makes a lot of work for the U.S. Postal Service.

Since Ruth and Walter are getting a refund, they sent in their tax return early. Now they're just waiting for their refund to come in the mail.

If you are getting a refund, it's better to send in your return early. But if you have to *pay* taxes, it's better to wait.

Why do so many people wait until the last minute to mail in their tax returns?

The mail brings a surprise

Walter is very excited. He found something very special in the mail today.

"It's here, Ruth!" Walter calls. "The return address says Internal Revenue Service! It's our tax refund!" He tries to tear open the envelope, but he can't get it open at first.

"I'm all thumbs," Walter says.

"Don't tear the check!" cries Ruth.

When was the last time you had a surprise in the mail?

Walter stops smiling

"No check!" shouts Walter. The IRS has not sent a refund check. The letter says that the Adamses are going to be audited. That means the IRS will check the Adamses' income tax return very carefully. The IRS wants to make sure that there are no mistakes.

Walter can't believe it. He thinks that he and Ruth did something wrong.

Why do you think the IRS audits tax returns?

The shoe box may save the day

Ruth tells Walter not to get upset. They didn't make any mistakes. They followed all the directions, line by line, on their tax return. They even have their shoe box full of sales slips to prove everything. The IRS just picks some returns each year to audit. This year Walter and Ruth got picked.

"We have nothing to worry about," says Walter. "Have we?"

How can Ruth and Walter get ready for the audit?

Walter shares his troubles with Frank

Walter is checking prices at Frank and Marge's store. Frank can see that Walter doesn't look happy.

"I've got tax troubles," says Walter. He tells Frank that Ruth isn't worried about being audited. But he is.

How would you feel about being audited?

Honest people shouldn't worry

"Ruth says that since we were honest, there's nothing to worry about," Walter says about the audit. "I guess she's right."

Then Frank tells Walter about his Uncle Jimmy. Uncle Jimmy was audited one time. It cost him ten years in jail.

"You're kidding!" shouts Walter. The idea of going to jail scares him.

Would Frank's story about being audited make you nervous?

Poor Uncle Jimmy

Frank says that Uncle Jimmy made a few mistakes on his tax return. The next thing he knew, he was in jail.

But Walter doesn't believe it. No one spends ten years in jail just for a few little mistakes.

"Uncle Jimmy did," Frank says. "He said that he made $6,000 from his flower shop. But the IRS found some money that he forgot to report."

Do you think that Frank should tell this story to Walter?

Walter doesn't think it's funny

Uncle Jimmy "forgot" to report more than a litle bit of money. He didn't report $30,000! Now Walter knows that Frank was only joking. But Walter isn't laughing. He is still going to be audited.

Frank tells him that audits are no big deal.

"You've got *nothing* to worry about," Frank tells him.

Why isn't Frank worried about Walter's audit?

The day has come

Walter and Ruth are in the IRS office for their audit. Walter is still nervous about it.

"Now don't worry," the auditor says. "There's nothing to this."

The IRS auditor isn't trying to make things difficult. He just wants to make sure that Walter and Ruth pay the right amount of taxes. Ruth and Walter might even get more money back than they had planned on.

Why is Walter nervous?

The shoe box gets around

The auditor is glad that Walter and Ruth saved their sales slips. Some people throw them away. Then they have no proof of their deductions.

Important records should be saved for three years. The IRS can call for an audit that far back. The auditor tells Walter and Ruth not to bring in more than the IRS asks for. Why give them something else to check?

Do you think that the auditor is trying to be helpful?

Walter has a question

The auditor is trying to be helpful. Ruth wonders whose side the auditor is on—theirs or the IRS's.

"We will tell you anything that will help you," the auditor explains.

"What happens if you find something wrong that we think is OK?" Walter asks.

How is this auditor different from what Ruth and Walter expected?

How fair is the IRS?

Then the auditor answers Walter's question. Suppose the IRS says you must pay more tax—but you don't agree. The auditor would take the case to his boss. Walter wonders if the boss would be fair. After all, both he and the auditor work for the IRS.

Sometimes the boss doesn't agree with the auditor. But if he did, Ruth and Walter could take the case to court. And they might win.

When do you think it would be worth fighting the IRS in court?

Frank falls for it

Frank sees Walter and Ruth coming into the store. He wants to know how the audit went.

"Frank, it was one of the worst things I've ever been through in my life," groans Walter. "We don't know where we'll get the money to pay the taxes that they say we owe."

When Ruth agrees, Frank starts to believe the story.

Why do you think that Walter plays this joke on Frank?

Ruth plays along

Then Marge comes into the store and asks about the audit.

Walter tells her it was really bad, too. Frank really believes Walter now. Then Frank walks away to take care of another customer.

When Frank leaves, Ruth lets Marge in on the joke.

Would you ever play a joke like this on someone?

Marge hears the real story

Ruth and Walter tell Marge what they learned at the IRS. You should file your tax return no matter what. If you can't pay your taxes, send in the return anyway. The IRS will give you time to pay. If you don't think you made enough money to pay taxes on, you should still send in a return.

Do you think the audit was a good thing for Ruth and Walter?

Mr. Shopper has something to say

Marge says that she could use some money back from taxes. She could also get money by selling Ruth some food. But Walter has been doing all the shopping. So Ruth asks him if she can buy food.

"I have something to say to you, Ruth," says Walter. He has done some thinking about comparison shopping. He knows it's a good way to save some money.

"But . . ." Walter says.

What do you think is on Walter's mind?

It's Ruth's turn

Walter has learned a lot about comparison shopping. He has been going to five stores to find the best prices. Later, Ruth goes back to buy the food. Walter says that he probably spends more money on gas than he saves on food! So Walter has decided to let Ruth do the grocery shopping again, as she used to.

But Ruth wants Walter to do *his* share, too. So they will take turns buying the food from now on.

Do you think that Ruth's idea will work?

Now it's Frank's turn

Frank has finished with his customer. Now he wants to know what happened to Ruth and Walter at the IRS. But he doesn't wait for an answer.

"I'd like to see them try something like that with *me*," says Frank. "*I*'d tell them a thing or two."

Then Marge hands him the mail. There is something from the IRS.

"Oh, no!" screams Frank. "It's . . . they want me for . . . an AUDIT!"

How do you think Frank feels about audits now?